Grandpa,
Why Do We Pray?

Carol Harblin

ISBN 979-8-88616-066-6 (paperback)
ISBN 979-8-88616-067-3 (digital)

Christian Faith Publishing
832 Park Avenue
Meadville, PA 16335
www.christianfaithpublishing.com

Printed in the United States of America

NJR, JLA, OMH, JTR

Lily Mae and her grandpa walked to church every Sunday. He wore his favorite blue necktie, and she wore her blue hair ribbons in her hair to match her grandpa.

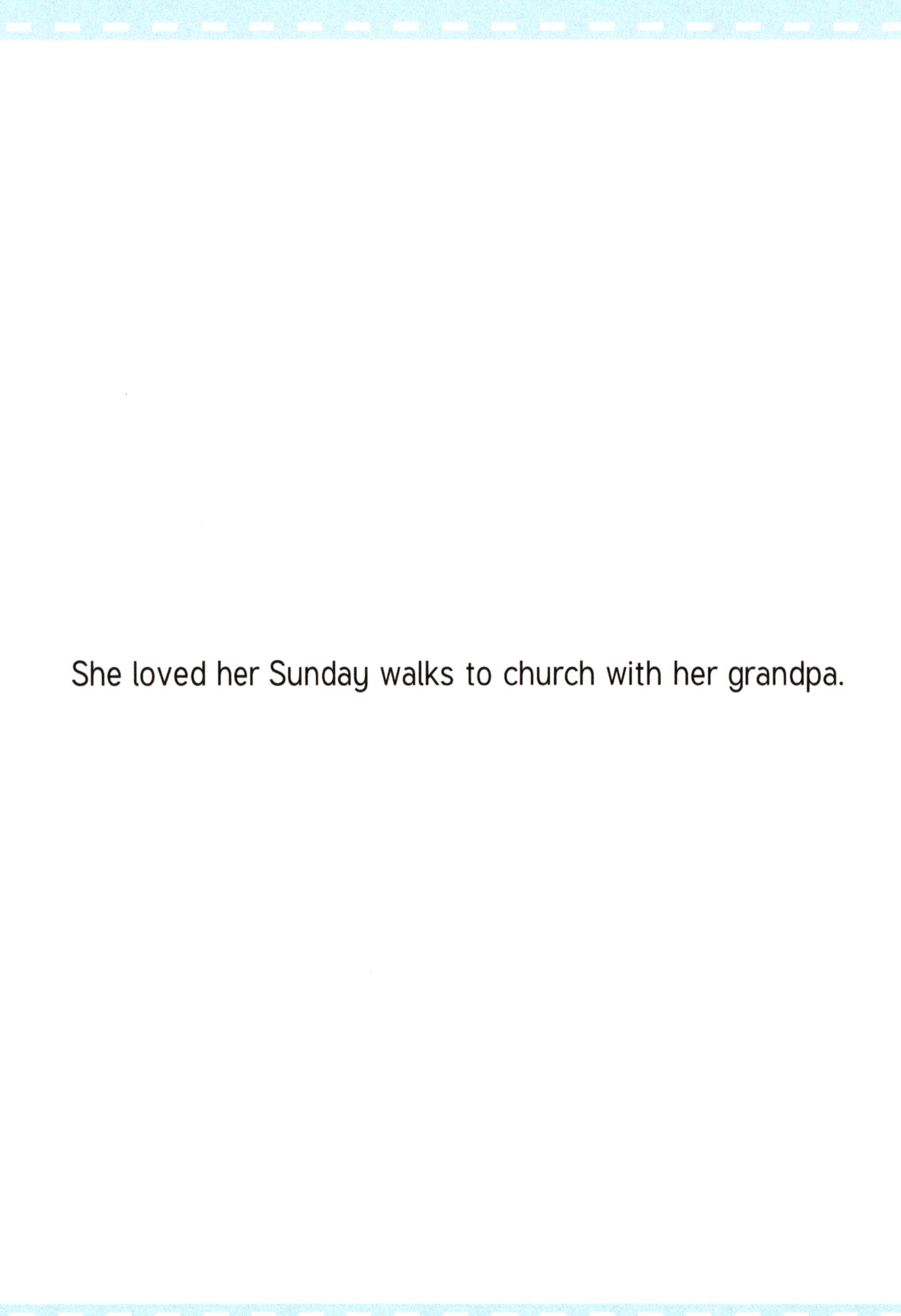

She loved her Sunday walks to church with her grandpa.

She held his hand as they walked, especially when they crossed the street. They explored nature as they walked together. She always asked him questions along the way.

"Look at that bird, Grandpa! Where does he go when it rains? What does he like to eat the most? Why do squirrels like to eat nuts?"

Another favorite game they played was to guess what the cloud formations looked like.

"Look at that cloud! It looks like a duck!" Lily Mae giggled. "What does it look like to you?" She asked.

"Looks like a rabbit or a slice of pizza with pepperoni!" Grandpa chuckled. He liked to guess two different answers just to make Lily Mae laugh and guess more.

They continued their walk.

Her grandpa patiently and thoughtfully answered her questions.

"I see the top of the church, Grandpa! We're getting closer!"
She looked up at him.
Finally, she asked the question she's wondered,
"Grandpa, why do we pray?"

"Oh, my darling Lily Mae, that is a great question," Grandpa said, "Praying is something we must do every day as a love for God and our family in heaven."

"But *why* do we pray?" asked Lily Mae again.

He thoughtfully considered his granddaughter. He wanted her to understand that praying wasn't something to do when you want something or when things are bad.

"Well, we brush our teeth to keep our teeth and gums healthy and strong... We eat breakfast for a healthy start of our day... We wash our hands throughout the day to protect ourselves from germs... And we pray for our health too, sweetheart!" He smiled. "It is important for our heart and soul... It keeps us from being alone in the world because we know we are connected to God and heaven...

"Heaven doesn't have phones like we have here at home, so we have to pray to talk to God and our family in heaven... We should always talk to God to let Him know how we are, not just when we need Him, but to talk, like we do...

"Pray when it rains, snows, and when it is sunny outside… Pray when you laugh and have a good day, just like when you pray when you have a bad day… God wants to hear from you always, my darling. God loves you.

"Do you only brush your teeth when you have a cavity or when you see the dentist? No. The same with praying. It's something to do every day."

"He's not too busy?" Lily Mae asked.

"God is never too busy for us, and He always wants us to check in all the time," Grandpa said. "He likes to hear from us every day, not just when we need something. God likes to be part of our daily routines. Don't just think of him when you want him. He isn't a genie or a wish factory."

Lily Mae nodded thoughtfully, "So it's like talkin' to you every day an' textin' Mommy an callin' Daddy when he is around the world?"

Grandpa smiled. "Yes, indeed."

Lily Mae and her grandpa finally arrived at church.

"Thank you." She hugged him. "I love you, Grandpa!"

Just then as Lily Mae looked up toward the sky, she saw bright sunbeams shoot out from the clouds.

"I love you too, God!"

Lily Mae and her grandpa stepped inside of the church.

"Thank you, Grandpa! Let's always pray and keep God company."

Grandpa smiled.

About the Author

Educator, author, and writer Carol Harblin journeyed around the world to India and Europe and throughout the United States, observing cultures and people through the eyes of a child. She sees the world with sincerity and unconditional love. She holds degrees from Iona University, Russell Sage College, and also her MFA from Goddard College. Carol's mission in life is to inspire, encourage, and motivate anyone who shows interest in her words and her heart. Carol is currently a professor and continues to write.

www.ingramcontent.com/pod-product-compliance
Lightning Source LLC
Chambersburg PA
CBHW041825110726
48006CB00019B/2510